SIGHT LINES

Books by Arthur Sze

ARTHUR SZE

Sight Lines

 Copper Canyon Press
Port Townsend, Washington

Cover art: Eve Aschheim, *Da Vinci's Circle,* 1989, graphite and
gesso on paper

Copper Canyon Press is in residence at Fort Worden State Park
in Port Townsend, Washington, under the auspices of Centrum.
Centrum is a gathering place for artists and creative thinkers
from around the world, students of all ages and backgrounds,
and audiences seeking extraordinary cultural enrichment.

LIBRARY OF CONGRESS CATALOGING-IN-PUBLICATION DATA
Names: Sze, Arthur, author.
Title: Sight lines / Arthur Sze.
Description: Port Townsend, Washington : Copper Canyon
    Press, [2019]
Identifiers: LCCN 2018052007 | ISBN 9781556595592 (paperback
    : alk. paper)
Classification: LCC PS3569.Z38 A6 2019 | DDC 811/.54—dc23
LC record available at https://lccn.loc.gov/2018052007

9 8 7 6 5 4 3 2   FIRST PRINTING

Copper Canyon Press
Post Office Box 271
Port Townsend, Washington 98368

www.coppercanyonpress.org

for Carol

Contents

SIGHT LINES

Water Calligraphy

1

A green turtle in broth is brought to the table—
I stare at an irregular formation of rocks

above a pond and spot, on the water's
surface, a moon. As I step back and forth,

the moon slides from partial to full
to partial and then into emptiness; but no

moon's in the sky, just slanting sunlight,
leafing willows along Slender West Lake,

parked cars outside an apartment complex
where, against a background of chirping birds

and car horns, two women bicker. Now
it's midnight at noon; I hear an electric saw

and the occasional sound of lumber striking
pavement. At the bottom of a teacup,

leaves form the character *individual*
and, after a sip, the number *eight*.

Snipped into pieces, a green turtle is returned
to the table; while everyone eats,

strands of thrown silk tighten, tighten
in my gut. I blink, and a woodblock carver

peels off pear shavings, stroke by stroke,
and foregrounds characters against empty space.

Begging in a subway, a blind teen and his mother stagger through the swaying car—

a woman lights a bundle of incense and bows at a cauldron—

people raise their palms around the Nine-Dragon Juniper—

who knows the mind of a watermelon vendor picking his teeth?—

you glance up through layers of walnut leaves in a courtyard—

biting into marinated lotus stems—

in a drum tower, hours were measured
as water rising then spilling from one kettle into another—

pomegranate trees flowering along a highway—

climbing to the top of a pagoda, you look down at rebuilt city walls—

a peacock cries—

always the clatter of mah-jongg tiles behind a door—

at a tower loom, a man and woman weave brocade silk—

squashing a cigarette above a urinal, a bus driver hurries back—

a musician strikes sticks, faster and faster—

cars honk along a street approaching a traffic circle—

when he lowers his fan, the actor's face has changed from black to white—

a child squats and shits in a palace courtyard—

yellow construction cranes pivot over the tops of high-rise apartments—

a woman throws a shuttle with green silk through the shed—

where are we headed, you wonder, as you pick a lychee and start to peel it—

3

Lightning ignites a fire in the wilderness: in hours,
200 then 2,000 acres are aflame; when a hotshot
crew hikes in to clear lines, a windstorm
kicks up and veers the blaze back, traps them,
and their fire shelters become their body bags.
Piñons in the hills have red and yellow needles—
in a bamboo park, a woman dribbles liquefied sugar
onto a plate, and it cools, on a stick, in the form
of a butterfly; a man in red pants stills
then moves through the Crane position.
A droplet hangs at the tip of a fern—water
spills into another kettle; you visualize
how flames engulfed them at 50 miles per hour.
In the West, wildfires scar each summer—
water beads on beer cans at a lunch counter—
you do not want to see exploding propane tanks;
you try to root in the world, but events sizzle
along razor wire, along a snapping end of a power line.

4

Two fawns graze on leaves in a yard—
as we go up the Pearl Tower, I gaze
through smog at freighters along the river.
A thunderstorm gathers: it rains and hails
on two hikers in the Barrancas; the arroyo
becomes a torrent, and they crouch for an hour.
After a pelting storm, you spark into flame
and draw the wax of the world into light—
ostrich and emu eggs in a basket by the door,
the aroma of cumin and pepper in the air.
In my mouth, a blister forms then disappears.
At a teak table, with family and friends,
we eat Dungeness crab, but, as I break
apart shell and claws, I hear a wounded elk
shot in the bosque. Canoers ask and receive
permission to land; they beach a canoe
with a yellow cedar wreath on the bow
then catch a bus to the fairgrounds powwow.

5

—Sunrise: I fill my rubber bucket with water
    and come to this patch of blue-gray sidewalk—
I've made a sponge-tipped brush at the end
    of a waist-high plastic stick; and, as I dip it,
I know water is my ink, memory my blood—

the tips of purple bamboo arch over the park—
    I see a pitched battle at the entrance to a palace
and rooftops issuing smoke and flames—
    today, there's a white statue of a human figure,
buses and cars drive across the blank square—

at that time, I researched carp in captivity
    and how they might reproduce and feed
people in communes—I might have made
    a breakthrough, but Red Guards knocked at the door—
they beat me, woke me up at all hours

until I didn't know whether it was midnight or noon—
    I saw slaughtered pigs piled on wooden racks,
snow in the spring sunshine—the confessions
    they handed me I signed—I just wanted it
to end—then herded pigs on a farm—wait—

a masseur is striking someone's back,
    his hands clatter like wooden blocks—
now I block the past by writing the present—
    as I write the strokes of *moon,* I let the brush
~~swerve~~ rest for a moment before I lift it

and make the one ~~stroke~~ hook—ah, it's all
    in that hook—there, I levitate: no mistakes
will last, even regret is lovely—my hand

trembles; but if I find the ~~gaps~~ resting places,
I cut the sinews of an ox, even as the ~~sun~~

moon waxes—the bones drop, my brush is sharp,
    sharper than steel—and though people murmur
at the evaporating characters, I smile, ~~frown~~
    fidget, let go—I draw the white, not the black—

6

Tea leaves in the cup spell *above* then *below*—
outside the kitchen window, a spray

of wisteria blossoms in May sunshine.
What unfolds inside us? We sit at a tabletop

that was once a wheel in Thailand: an iron hoop
runs along the rim. On a fireplace mantel,

a flame flickers at the bottom of a metal cup.
As spokes to a hub, a chef cleans blowfish:

turtles beach on white sand: a monk rakes
gravel into scalloped waves in a garden:

moans issue from an alley where men stir
from last night's binge. If all time converges

as light from stars, all situations reside here.
In red-edged heat, I irrigate the peach trees;

you bake a zucchini frittata; water buffalo
browse in a field; hail has shredded lettuces,

and, as a farmer paces and surveys damage,
a coyote slips across a road, under barbed wire.

7

The letter A was once an inverted cow's head,
but now, as I write, it resembles feet
planted on the earth rising to a point.

Once is glimpsing the Perseid meteor shower—
and, as emotion curves space, I find
a constellation that arcs beyond the visible.

A neighbor brings cucumbers and basil;
when you open the bag and inhale, the world
inside is fire in a night courtyard

at summer solstice; we have limned the time here
and will miss the bamboo arcing along
the fence behind our bedroom, peonies

leaning to earth. A *mayordomo* retrenches
the opening to the ditch; water runs near
the top of juniper poles that line our length—

in the bosque, the elk carcass decomposes
into a stench of antlers and bones. Soon
ducks will nest on the pond island, and as

a retired violinist who fed skunks left a legacy—
one she least expected—we fold this
in our pocket and carry it wherever we go.

Stilling to North

Just as the blue tip of a compass needle
stills to north, you stare at a pencil

with sharpened point, a small soapstone
bear with a tiny chunk of turquoise

tied to its back, the random pattern
of straw flecked in an adobe wall;

you peruse the silver poplar branches,
the spaces between branches, and as

a cursor blinks, situate at the edge
of loss—the axolotl was last sighted

in Xochimilco over twenty years ago;
a jaguar meanders through tawny

brush in the Gila Wilderness—
and, as the cursor blinks, you guess

it's a bit of line that arcs—a parsec
made visible—and as you sit,

the imperfections that mark you
attune you to a small emptied flask

tossed to the roadside and the X,
never brewed, that throbs in your veins.

—No one could anticipate this distance from Monticello—

Westbourne Street

Porch light illuminating white steps, light
   over a garage door, darkness inside windows—
and the darkness exposes the tenuous.
   A glassblower shapes a rearing horse
that shifts, on a stand, from glowing orange
   to glistening crystal; suddenly the horse

shatters into legs, head, body, mane.
   At midnight, "Fucking idiot!" a woman yells,
shaking the house; along a hedge,
   a man sleeps, coat over head, legs sticking out;
and, at 8 a.m., morning glories open
   on a fence; a backhoe heads up the street.

From this window, he views banana leaves,
   an orange tree with five oranges, houses
with shingled roofs, and steps leading
   to an upstairs apartment; farther off, palm trees,
and, beyond, a sloping street, ocean, sky;
   but what line of sight leads to revelation?

Cloud Hands

A woman moves through a Cloud Hands position,
          holding and rotating

an invisible globe—thud, shattering glass, moan,
          horn blast—so many

worlds to this world—two men dipnet
          sockeye salmon

at the mouth of a river—from a rooftop, a seagull
          squawks and cries;

a woman moves through Grasp the Bird's Tail—
          someone on a stretcher

is wheeled past glass doors—a desert fivespot
          rises in a wash—

and, pressing her tongue to the roof
          of her mouth,

she focuses, in the near distance, on the music
          of sycamore leaves.

In the Bronx

Crossing a street, you hear the cry of a strawberry finch,
        and, reaching the curb,

catch the smell of a young pig that, minutes ago,
        hurtled across the trail;

inhaling a chocolate scent, you approach a small orchid;
        nearby, two streaked

pitcher plants have opened lids but opened laterally;
        a fern rises out

of the crotch of an ʻōhiʻa tree, and droplets have collected
        on a mule's foot fern;

up on the ridge, sliding mist veils the palms and eucalyptus;
        nearby, a trumpet tree

dangles orange-scented blooms; you stare at the crack
        in a blue marble tree,

at a maze of buttressed roots, just as a man holding
        a placard, waving people

toward a new doughnut shop, turns and, thud, a wild avocado
        has dropped to the ground.

Unpacking a Globe

I gaze at the Pacific and don't expect
to ever see the heads on Easter Island,

though I guess at sunlight rippling
the yellow grasses sloping to shore;

yesterday a doe ate grass in the orchard:
it lifted its ears and stopped eating

when it sensed us watching from
a glass hallway—in his sleep, a veteran

sweats, defusing a land mine.
On the globe, I mark the Battle of

the Coral Sea—no one frets at that now.
A poem can never be too dark,

I nod and, staring at the Kenai, hear
ice breaking up along an inlet;

yesterday a coyote trotted across
my headlights and turned his head

but didn't break stride; that's how
I want to live on this planet:

alive to a rabbit at a glass door—
and flower where there is no flower.

—During the Cultural Revolution, a boy saw his mother shot by a firing squad—

Traversal

At dawn you dip oars in water, row out
        on a lake—the oarlocks creak—and, drifting,

inhale the pines along the shore. A woman
        puts water in a pot, lights a stove: before

it steams, she looks out at the glimmering:
        between two points, we traverse an infinite set

of paths: here we round a bend in an arroyo
        and stumble onto two sheep carcasses;

here peonies and ranunculus unfold in a vase.
        The day has the tensile strength of silk:

you card the hours, spin them, dip
        the skeins in a dye pot, and grief or anger,

pleasure or elation's the mordant that fixes
        the hue. You find yourself stepping

through a T-shaped doorway: the niches
        in a circular ruin mark the sun's motion;

a woman fries potatoes in a pan and finds,
        in the night, mice have slipped through

a hole under the sink and nibbled soap
        in a dish; a returning hunter pulls a screen

latch but, hearing a rattlesnake inside,
        slams it, stares through the vibrating mesh.

The Radiant's

the origin point of a meteor shower.
     Peaches redden: branches
          are propped with juniper posts

and a shovel; steam rises
     from a caldera; stepping
          through a lava tube, we emerge

into a rain forest dotted
     with wild ginger; desire
          branches like mycelium.

Carrying a bolete in a basket,
     we forage under spruce and fir
          in cool alpine air;

a plume rises where lava reaches
     the ocean. Who said, *Out of nothing,*
          nothing can come? We do not lie

in a meadow to view the Perseids
     but discover, behind a motel,
          a vineyard, and gather as we go.

Doppler Effect

Stopped in cars, we are waiting to accelerate
along different trajectories. I catch the rising

pitch of a train—today one hundred nine people
died in a stampede converging at a bridge;

radioactive water trickles underground
toward the Pacific Ocean; nickel and copper

particulates contaminate the Brocade River.
Will this planet sustain ten billion people?

Ah, switch it: a spider plant leans toward
a glass door, and six offshoots dangle from it;

the more I fingered the clay slab into a bowl,
the more misshapen it became; though I have

botched *this,* bungled *that,* the errancies
reveal it would not be better if things happened

just as I wished; a puffer fish inflates on deck;
a burst of burnt rubber rises from pavement.

Adamant

Deer browse at sunrise in an apple orchard,
while honey locust leaves litter the walk.
A neighbor hears gunshots in the bosque

and wonders who's firing at close range;
I spot bear prints near the Pojoaque River
but see no sign of the reported mountain lion.

As chlorophyll slips into the roots of a cottonwood
and the leaves burst into yellow-gold, I wonder,
where's our mortal flare? You can travel

to where the Tigris and Euphrates flow together
and admire the inventions of people living
on floating islands of reeds; you can travel

along an archipelago and hike among volcanic
pools steaming with water and sulfuric acid;
but you can't change the eventual, adamant body.

Though death might not come like a curare-
dipped dart blown out of a tube or slam
at you like surf breaking over black lava rock,

it will come—it *will* come—and it unites us—
brother, sister, boxer, spinner—in this pact,
while you inscribe a letter with trembling hand.

—A woman detonates when a spam text triggers bombs strapped to her body—

Python Skin

1

Smoke engulfs a boat in the harbor—we motor
      past and recall a flotilla of fishing boats

lashed together and Hong Kong skyscrapers
      in the distance—when we dock, I continue

to bob and smell diesel fumes on water;
      though medical researchers extract saliva

from Gila monsters, draw blue blood
      from horseshoe crabs, seeding a cloud

is never a cure; on a fireplace mantel,
      a flame sways then steadies above a pool

of wax, and a tuberose aroma fills the room;
      at sunrise, I spot a grapevine leafing out:

though no coyote slants across the field
      with a rabbit in its mouth, though no grenade

is hurled over here, I recall fires crackling
      in jagged lines along a ridge to the west,

apple trees out the window vanishing in smoke—
      haze wherever we look, think, run, stop, be.

2

Beer bottles and diapers thrown out of car windows—
    you carry a shovel down to the cattail pond where,
each spring, someone cuts a channel and drains
    water into the nearby acequia; you patch the channel
but know by summer it will be cut open again;

no one ever knows who does this; you never meet
    the lab technician who works on bombs—*I work
on sound: sound waves are odd when they
    turn a corner, and their wavelengths stretch,*
and you compartmentalize and list your errands:

post office, meeting with water lawyer, buy apples
    and yogurt for lunch; and barely notice a hummingbird
darting from columbine to columbine; an accountant
    yearns to stroll in a meadow, inhale the alpine
air, listen to water cascading between rocks,

but he squints at numbers in columns; and a lawyer
    dates his boss but one day he handcuffs and assaults her,
breaks two bones in her face as she begs for her life—
    in jail he takes the prison razor given him to shave,
disassembles it, then slits his throat in the night.

3

The housewives of Königsberg set their kitchen
clocks to when a philosopher walked by the window;

a daily timed walk is a single violin string
out of which all waves rise and fall—deep-fried

crabs are immersed in a basket of Sichuan chiles;
at a subway juncture, a man bows an erhu,

and a melody reverberates down the walkways;
the outlines of branches emerge out of the dark—

I peruse the pale eyes of a cuttlefish crammed
into a tank: what if you ask the vibrating

python skin of an erhu how it feels to make sound—
what if salt or a lichen or the erhu spoke?

4

A cat drops a downy woodpecker at the door—
        one day a man wakes to a pain in his chest
and requires a quadruple bypass—he eats
        frybread for lunch; you scan a black
locust whose last branch failed to leaf this spring;

though acknowledging grief assuages the pain,
        red dye droplets splash into water and swirl
before vanishing from sight; though the locust
        will be stacked as firewood, you observe mounds
ants make in the courtyard and recognize how

their channels of empty spaces extend vital breath;
        you do not sense impending doom but deep-
water the cottonwood that survived a drought
        and shades the house; in an erhu melody
filling the subway walkway, you catch the tremor

of python skin but apprehend another python
        snag on a branch and peel off a layer;
as the two strings evoke shadows of candles
        flickering red, you gather wild irises
out of the air and peel off *mine, yours, his, hers:*

5

flitting to the honeysuckle, a white butterfly—

when she scribbles a few phrases by candlelight, a peony buds—

two does bound up from the apple orchard—

he sprays a paper-wasp nest under the portal—

sunlight touches the highest leaves of the silver poplars—

a buck scrapes his rack on a slender aspen trunk—

you slow but drive steadily through a hailstorm until it clears—

walkingstick on the screen door—

swimming back to shore, they spot a few turtles in the shallows—

we stroll up an arroyo then glance back at the S-curve of trees in the valley—

the steady hum of cars driving men to the lab—

red-winged blackbirds nesting in the cattails—

here a peony buds and fragrances the air—

he kisses the back of her neck, and she nestles along his body—

in the sky, not a shred of cloud—

Lichen Song

—Snow in the air   you've seen a crust on the ceiling wood and
never considered how I gather moisture when you step out of the
shower   you don't care that I respire as you breathe   for years
you've washed your face gazed in the mirror shaved combed
your hair rushed out while I who may grow an inch in a thou-
sand years catch the tingling sunlight   you don't understand
how I can dive to a temperature of liquefied gas and warm back
up absorb water start growing again without a scar   I can float
numb in space be hit with cosmic rays then return to Earth and
warm out of my sleep to respire again without a hiccup   you
come and go while I stay gripped to pine and the sugar of exis-
tence runs through you runs through me you sliver if you just
go go go   if you slowed you could discover that mosquitoes bat
their wings six hundred times a second and before they mate
synchronize their wings you could feel how they flicker with
desire   I am flinging your words and if you absorb not blot my
song you could learn you are not alone in pain and grief though
you've instilled pain and grief   you can urge the dare and thrill
of bliss if and when you stop to look at a rock at a fence post
but you cough only look yes look at me now because you are blink
about to leave—

Black Center

Green tips of tulips are rising out of the earth—
you don't flense a whale or fire at beer cans

in an arroyo but catch the budding
tips of pear branches and wonder what

it's like to live along a purling edge of spring.
Jefferson once tried to assemble a mastodon

skeleton on the White House floor but,
with pieces missing, failed to sequence the bones;

when the last speaker of a language dies,
a hue vanishes from the spectrum of visible light.

Last night, you sped past revolving and flashing
red, blue, and white lights along the road—

a wildfire in the dark; though no one
you knew was taken in the midnight ambulance,

an arrow struck a bull's-eye and quivered
in its shaft: one minute gratitude rises

like water from an underground lake;
another, dissolution gnaws from a black center.

Under a Rising Moon

Driving at night between Chinle and Tsaile,
I fixate on deer along the road: in the headlights,
they're momentarily blinded but could leap out.
An unglazed pot fired and streaked from ash
will always bear the beauty of chance, while
a man who flies by helicopter and lands
on an iceberg will always bear the crunching
sounds under his feet. This morning we hiked
from the rim down to White House Ruins,
and the scraping of cottonwood leaves
is still in my ears. *Diné women tied their infants*
on cradleboards, stashed them in crevices
but never came back. Though warned of elk,
I heed the car with a single headlight enlarging
in my rearview mirror—when the mind
is sparked with pixels, it's hard to swerve
and brake. The Anasazi must have marveled
at the whitening sheen on the cliff, but tonight
tracks of moonlight run ahead of where I can be.

Light Echoes

In the parking lot, we look up at the Milky Way:
a poacher aims a rifle at a black rhinoceros:

a marble boat disappears in smog.
As I gaze at an anthurium, wild cockatoos

cry from the tops of blue marble trees;
a lake forms on an ice sheet: rivers branch

and branch. A guitarist leans into the space
between notes; a stone plummets

down a black well: he does not know
the silence when he will aim a bullet

at himself. On a wall, a red spider;
macaws in cages squawk when we approach:

I scratch letters into the leaf of an autograph tree.
Like lights extending along a bay,

notes from Norteña splay in my ears—
they sparkle then disappear into black sounds.

First Snow

A rabbit has stopped on the gravel driveway:

> imbibing the silence,
> you stare at spruce needles:

>> there's no sound of a leaf blower,
>> no sign of a black bear;

a few weeks ago, a buck scraped his rack
> against an aspen trunk;
> a carpenter scribed a plank along a curved stone wall.

> You only spot the rabbit's ears and tail:

when it moves, you locate it against speckled gravel,
but when it stops, it blends in again;

> the world of being is like this gravel:

>> you think you own a car, a house,
>> this blue-zigzagged shirt, but you just borrow these things.

Yesterday, you constructed an aqueduct of dreams
> and stood at Gibraltar,
>> but you possess nothing.

Snow melts into a pool of clear water;
> and, in this stillness,

>> starlight behind daylight wherever you gaze.

—Salt cedar rises through silt in an irrigation ditch—

Courtyard Fire

At autumn equinox,
    we make a fire
        in the courtyard: sparks

gust into the black air,
    and all seasons are enfolded
        in these flames:

snow gathers and tips the lilac twigs;
    a stinkhorn rises
        out of dirt below a waterspout;

ants climb the peony stalks;
    and, gazing into coals,
        I skydive and pass through

stages of youth: at first,
    I climb a tower and,
        looking out, find the world tipped;

then I dash through halls:
    if ripening is all,
        what can the dead teach us?

We who must rage and lust,
    hurtle zigzagging between cars
        in traffic, affirm

the call to abandon illusions
    is a call to abandon
        a condition that requires illusions;

and, as I pull the cord,
    spring rips and blooms;
        on landing, I sway on earth.

White Sands

—Walking along a ridge of white sand—
                        it's cooler below the surface—

we stop and, gazing at an expanse
        of dunes to the west,
                watch a yellow yolk of sun drop to the mountains—

an hour earlier, we rolled down a dune,
                    white sand flecked your eyelids and hair—

a claret cup cactus blooms,
           and soaptree yuccas
                      move as a dune moves—

so many years later, on a coast, waves rolling to shore,
                wave after wave,

I see how our lives have unfolded,
              a sheen of
                  wave after whitening wave—

and we are stepping barefoot,
           rolling down a dune, white flecks on our lips,

on our eyelids: we are lying in a warm dune
                as a full moon
                      lifts against an ocean of sky—

Salt Song

Zunis make shrines on the way to a lake where I emerge   and
Miwoks gather me out of pools along the Pacific   the cheetah
thirsts for me   and when you sprinkle me on rib eye you have
no idea how I balance silence with thunder in crystal   you
dream of butterfly hunting in Madagascar   spelunking through
caves echoing with dripping stalactites   and you don't see how
I yearn to shimmer an orange aurora against flame   look at
me in your hand   in Egypt I scrubbed the bodies of kings and
queens   in Pakistan I zigzag upward through twenty-six miles
of tunnels before drawing my first breath in sunlight   if you
heat a kiln to 2380 degrees and scatter me inside   I vaporize
and bond with clay   in this unseen moment a potter prays
because my pattern is out of his hands   and when I touch your
lips   you salivate   and when I dissolve on your tongue   your
hair rises   ozone unlocks   a single stroke of lightning sizzles
to earth.

—The plutonium waste has been hauled to an underground site—

Sprang

1 WINTER STARS

You will never forget corpses wrapped in flames—
at dusk, you watched a congregation of crows

gather in the orchard and sway on branches;
in the dawn light, a rabbit moves and stops,

moves and stops along the grass; and as
you pull a newspaper out of a box, glance

at the headlines, you feel the dew on grass
as the gleam of fading stars: yesterday you met

a body shop owner whose father was arrested,
imprisoned, and tortured in Chile, heard

how men were scalded to death in boiling water;
and, as the angle of sunlight shifts, you feel

a seasonal tilt into winter with its expanse
of stars—candles flickering down the Ganges,

where you light a candle on a leaf and set it
flickering, downstream, into darkness—

dozens of tiny flames flickering into darkness—
then you gaze at fires erupting along the shore.

2   HOLE

No sharp-shinned hawk perches
on the roof rack of his car and scans
for songbirds; the reddening ivy
along a stone wall deepens in hue;
when he picks a sungold tomato
in the garden and savors
the burst in his mouth, he catches
a mock orange spray in the air;
and as he relights the pilot
to a water heater, checks thermostats,
the sound of water at a fountain
is prayer; earlier in the summer,
he watched a hummingbird land,
sip water, and douse its wings,
but, now, a widening hole gnaws
at that time; and, glancing
at a spotted towhee nest on a lintel,
he knows how hunting chanterelles
at the ski basin and savoring
them at dinner is light-years away.

3 TALISMAN

Quetzal: you write
    the word on a sheet of paper
        then erase it;

each word, a talisman,
    leaves a track: a magpie
        struts across a portal

and vanishes from sight;
    when you bite into sea urchin,
        ocean currents burst

in your mouth; and when
    you turn, view the white shutters
        to the house,

up the canyon, a rainbow
    arcs into clouds;
        expectancies, fears, yearnings—

hardly bits of colored glass
    revolving in a kaleidoscope—
        mist rising from a hot spring

along a river: suddenly
    you are walking toward Trinity Site
        searching for glass

and counting minutes
    of exposure under the sun;
        suddenly small things ignite.

4   *KINTSUGI*

He slips on ice near a mailbox—

no gemsbok leaps across the road—

a singer tapped an eagle feather on his shoulders—

women washed indigo-dyed yarn in this river, but today gallium and germanium
    particles are washed downstream—

once they dynamited dikes to slow advancing troops—

picking psilocybin mushrooms and hearing cowbells in the mist—

as a child, he was tied to a sheep and escaped marauding soldiers—

an apple blossom opens to five petals—

as he hikes up a switchback, he remembers undressing her—

from the train window, he saw they were on ladders cutting fruit off cacti—

in the desert, a crater of radioactive glass—

assembling shards, he starts to repair a gray bowl with gold lacquer—

they ate psilocybin mushrooms, gazed at the pond, undressed—

hunting a turkey in the brush, he stops—

from the ponderosa pines: *whoo-ah, whoo whoo whoo—*

5 YELLOW LIGHTNING

In the 5 a.m. dark, a car with bright lights
and hazard lights blinking drives directly at me;
veering across the yellow lines, I pass by it

and exhale: amethyst crystals accrete
on a string: I will live to see pear
blossoms in the orchard, red-winged black-

birds nesting in the cattails; I love the sighs
you make when you let go—my teeth gripping
your earlobe—pearls of air rising through water—

and as a white moon rising over a canyon
casts pine shadows to the ground, gratitude
rivers through me: sharpened to starlight,

I make our bed and find your crystal
between the sheets; and when I part the curtains,
daylight's a strobe of yellow lightning.

6 RED-RUFFED LEMUR

You locate a spotted towhee nest on a beam,
peony shoots rising out of the earth, but a pang
surges in your blood with each systole—
though spring emerges, the forsythia eludes you—
in a coffee shop, a homeless man gathers
a Chinese magazine and two laundered towels
in a clear plastic bag, mutters "Metro,"
and heads out the door—a bird trills
in the blue spruce, but when it stops, the silence
is water running out of thawing glacial ice;
and you mix cement in a wheelbarrow,
haul it, in a bucket, up a ladder to a man
on a rooftop plastering a parapet—cherry buds
unfurl along a tidal basin—a red-ruffed
lemur squints out of a cage at human faces,
shudders, and scurries back into a hole—
and you surge at what's enfolded in this world:

red bougainvillea blooming against the glass—

she likes it when he pulls her to him—

once you saw murres crowding the cliffs of an arctic island—

thousands of blue-black mussels, exposed and gripping rocks at low tide—

he runs his fingers between her toes—

light reflecting off snow dazzles their eyes—

a tiger shark prowls along the shoreline for turtles—

an aspen leaf drops into a creek—

when he tugs the roots of her hair, he begins to tiger—

this is the writing, the speaking of the dream—

no one knows why ten thousands of murres are dying—

he hungers for sunlight to slant along their bodies on a Moloka'i slope—

sunlight streams as gold-flecked koi roil the waters and churn—

they roil the waters and churn—

killer whales move through Prince William Sound—

8   NET LIGHT

Poised on a bridge, streetlights
on either shore, a man puts
a saxophone to his lips, coins
in an upturned cap, and a carousel

in a piazza begins to turn:
where are the gates to paradise?
A woman leans over an outstretched
paper cup—leather workers sew

under lamps: a belt, wallet, purse—
leather dyed maroon, beige, black—
workers from Seoul, Lagos, Singapore—
a fresco on a church wall depicts

the death of a saint: a friar raises
both hands in the air—on an airplane,
a clot forms in a woman's leg
and starts to travel toward her heart—

a string of notes riffles the water;
and, as the clot lodges, at a market
near lapping waves, men unload
sardines in a burst of argentine light.

9   SPRANG

Before tracking pods of killer whales
in Prince William Sound, she reads a poem

on deck to start each day. In solstice light,
a moose lumbers across a driveway; I mark

orange and purple sea stars exposed at low tide,
the entrance to an octopus den. Astronomers

have observed two black holes colliding;
and, though the waves support relativity,

we need no equation to feel the sprang of space
and time. A marine biologist gives everything

away, weaves her coffin out of alder branches,
lines it with leaves; a carpenter saws kiln-

dried planks to refurbish a porch; I peruse
the tips of honeycrisp apples we planted

last fall, and, though no blossoming appears,
the air is rife with it; the underground

stirs, and I can only describe it by saying
invisible deer move through an orchard in bloom.

—A man who built plutonium triggers breeds horses now—

Transfigurations

Though neither you nor I saw flowering pistachio trees
in the Hanging Gardens of Babylon, though neither
you nor I saw the Tigris River stained with ink,
though we never heard a pistachio shell dehisce,
we have taken turns holding a panda as it munched
on bamboo leaves, and I know that rustle now.
I have awakened beside you and inhaled August
sunlight in your hair. I've listened to the scroll
and unscroll of your breath—dolphins arc along
the surface between white-capped waves; here,
years after we sifted yarrow and read from the *Book
of Changes*, I mark the dissolving hues in the west
as the sky brightens above overhanging willows.
The panda fidgets as it pushes a stalk farther
into its mouth. We step into a clearing with budding
chanterelles; and, though this space shrinks and
is obscured in the traffic of a day, *here* is the anchor
I drop into the depths of teal water. I gaze deeply
at the panda's black patches around its eyes;
how did it evolve from carnivore to eater of bamboo?
So many transfigurations I will never fathom.
The arc of our lives is a brightening then dimming,
brightening then dimming—a woman catches
fireflies in an orchard with the swish of a net.
I pick an openmouthed pistachio from a bowl
and crack it apart: a hint of Assyria spills
into the alluvial fan of sunlight. I read spring in
autumn in the scroll of your breath; though
neither you nor I saw the completion of the Great Wall,
I wake to the unrepeatable contour of this breath.

Dawn Redwood

Early morning light: a young red-tailed hawk
    glided onto an overhead branch and peered

down at me, but it did not look with your eyes—
    a battered and rusted pickup lies in the wash;

Navajo tea buds on the trail—I headed back
    and checked, in the boiler room, the traps,

baited with peanut butter—now a gnat
    flits against this lit screen: where are you now?

One morning, we walked in a Rhode Island
    cemetery and did not look at a single gravestone;

we looked at hundred-year-old copper beeches,
    cells burnished purple, soaking up sunshine,

and talked about the dawn redwood,
    how the glimmering light at the beginning

of the world was in all things. This morning,
    in the predawn darkness, Orion angled

in the eastern sky with Sirius, low,
    above the ridgeline; and, before daylight

blotted out the stars, I heard you speak,
    the scratched words return to their sleeves.

Xeriscape

When she hands you a whale vertebra,
you marvel at its heft, at a black

pebble lodged in a lateral nook;
the hollyhocks out the window

stretch into sunshine; a dictionary
in the room is open to *xeriscape;*

the sidewalk and gravel heat all day
and release warmth into the night;

the woman who sits and writes
sees pressed aspen board, framers

setting window headers and door-
jambs—here no polar bears rummage

at the city dump, no seal-oil lamps
flicker in the tide of darkness—

you know the influx of afternoon
clouds, thunder, ball lightning,

wavering lines of rain that evaporate
before they strike the ground,

as you carefully set the whale bone
on the glass table next to the television.

The Far Norway Maples

Silver poplars rise and thin to the very twig,
but what thins at your fingertips?

The aspirations of a minute, a day, a year?
Yellow tangs veer in the water and, catching

sunlight, veer again, disappear from sight.
The unfolding of a life has junctures

that rupture plot: a child folds paper
and glues toothpicks, designs a split-level

house with white walls and pitched roof,
but his father snatches the maquette

and burns it. If you inhale and spore this moment,
it tumors your body, but if you exhale it,

you dissolve midnight and noon; sunlight
tilts and leafs the tips of the far Norway maples.

Sight Lines

I'm walking in sight of the Río Nambé—

salt cedar rises through silt in an irrigation ditch—

the snowpack in the Sangre de Cristos has already dwindled before spring—

at least no fires erupt in the conifers above Los Alamos—

the plutonium waste has been hauled to an underground site—

a man who built plutonium triggers breeds horses now—

no one could anticipate this distance from Monticello—

Jefferson despised newspapers, but no one thing takes us out of ourselves—

during the Cultural Revolution, a boy saw his mother shot by a firing squad—

a woman detonates when a spam text triggers bombs strapped to her body—

when I come to an upright circular steel lid, I step out of the ditch—

I step out of the ditch but step deeper into myself—

I arrive at a space that no longer needs autumn or spring—

I find ginseng where there is no ginseng my talisman of desire—

though you are visiting Paris, you are here at my fingertips—

though I step back into the ditch, no whitening cloud dispels this world's mystery—

the ditch ran before the year of the Louisiana Purchase—

I'm walking on silt, glimpsing horses in the field—

fielding the shapes of our bodies in white sand—

though parallel lines touch in the infinite, the infinite is here—

The Glass Constellation

Apple branches whiten in moonlight;

no god with an ibis head and human
body writes on a papyrus scroll here;

in daylight, snow has accumulated
on flagstone and fence posts; for days,

masons cut bricks on the patio:

the sound of a circular saw
echoed in your ears, but now scattered

husks of silence lie on the ground;
in a bowl-shaped fountain, water

rises and brims: if all time brims

at this threshold, a man tosses a beer
can out of a car then wrist-flicks a match:

a brush fire ignites, fans east
across a field toward a house and barn;

as the stench of smoke permeates

your clothes and hair, you lean on a shovel:
brush crackles then bursts into flame.

Shoveling snow off a patio, you spot ice
crystals, run your eyes along the glinting—

a varied thrush swallows a juniper berry;

from the air, we track migrating caribou,
and their shifting bodies make visible

the magnetic lines of the moment;
a magpie hops onto an apple-tree stump,

flies to a fence post, up to a branch;

you want that absorption, that vitality
when you turn a key at the door, step inside;

you consider what you've botched:
once you shortened a one-by-eight

so that you could level sand on a portal,

but the foreman stopped and screamed,
"You just sawed off my straightedge!"

Heat waves ripple up from a highway
outside a grapefruit farm near Salton Sea—

the road dissolves into shimmering sand;

you resume shoveling snow off
the walkway and tingle at the hot and cold:

once, in the dark, a large doe stood
behind you—a woman begs outside

the bakery—when he unlatched the gate,

fawns appeared in the orchard—
a temblor torqued the dining room

and silenced the laughter—a spotted towhee
lands on a nest and feeds her fledglings—

gazing into the vortex of the white page:

no jackal-headed god needs to weigh
your heart against an eagle feather—

at sunrise you divert water from the ditch
to sprinklers that swish, spray

the grass—a soldier on point pauses—

who knows the path of a man on crutches
begging at a stoplight?—from the under-

ground uranium mine, a shock wave
shattered windows in the village above—

in the dictionary, you open to *cochlea*

then *pungent*—a thinning membrane,
the earth's atmosphere—you write *respire*

then listen: nibbling dandelion stalks,
a cottontail—as peonies unfold

in a vase, you smell the back of her neck.

Researchers train honeybees, tagged
with microtransmitters, to track TNT

and locate land mines in fields;
Sun Tzu wrote, *to win one hundred*

victories in one hundred battles

is not the acme of skill; in the boiler room,
a plumber replaced a zone valve

but inadvertently let air into the water
line; at midnight, in a house

with no heat, you restart the boiler,

but, on the concrete floor, rat shit
is scattered like rice—though you set

a trap with peanut butter, you recall
a coyote munching an apple core,

gazing through the kitchen window,

unblinking in sunlight; a magpie
lands on a buck and eats ticks;

Sun Tzu wrote, *musical notes are only
five in number but their melodies*

are so numerous one cannot hear them all.

Nasturtium and lobelia planted in pots—
in the silence, a pipa twangs—a cougar

stalks neighborhood dogs in the dark—
you walked up to the acequia

but, finding no water, fingered the silt—

a sniper fires from a second-story window—
fingers start rolling and halting on strings—

where did I put my car keys—I'm ~~pissed~~ late—
what's this ~~fucking~~ note under the door—

behind on my rent?—that sound of a truck

~~coming down the street~~—I need a shot—
not yet—ugh—that sound of glass

breaking—now ~~piss me off~~ I have
to wait until that truck's gone—~~maybe~~

~~I'll move to Denver~~—to back out—

when the caribou arrive, flowering herbs
are starting to wilt—when you type

I have taken too little care— you step
out on a glacial lake at ten below:

ice crystals singe your eyelashes—

you mark the forking branches
of a tree in the darkening air;

minute by minute, your sight shrinks
and shallows until the glass panes

of the door shift from window to mirror;

at that moment, grief and joy tip the ends
of a scale; earlier, you did not know

you would live to see a blue gentian
flower out of air; so often you knew

the page before it burst into flame—

staring at the snowy field of the page,
you tense when an arctic fox

slips past the black trunks of trees:
you blink, and nothing is there;

the blinking cursor marks a pendulum

swinging from a vaulted ceiling
over a marble floor; though no god

fingers your nerves, you write *tingle*
and tingle as sleet turns to rain.

In the white space a poppy buds—

he runs his fingers through her hair—
the spray of mock orange streams by—

at a fountain, a spotted towhee sips—
clenching his hand, he tugs the roots

of her hair—a fisherman unspools a line

back and forth—relaxes his grip—
a fly drops onto a stream, and a cutthroat

snags it—unfolds a sky-blue poppy—
she is rubbing oil on his chest and nipples—

staccato lightning to the west—

swimming in the Pacific, they look
at two lines of dolphins undulating below—

encircling, one suddenly flips
into the air then plunges into the depths—

sound of a car shifting gears—out of PVC

pipes, water gushes into the orchard—
women are rinsing indigo-dyed yarn

in a river—he sees the zigzag blue
lines in tiles above the fireplace as he has

never seen them before—she sees June

light slanting through glass into the hallway—
before his ashes are scattered at sea,

you stare at a dead apricot tree in moonlight:
what was it like to hear a commotion

in the street and glimpse the last emperor

leave the Forbidden City? Years later,
in West Virginia, coal miners, armed

with sticks of dynamite, rolled on cots
into mine openings and then back out—

detonations in the past are laced

in garlic now; sniffing the air
and leaning his head back and forth,

a coyote trots by the glass door;
last night, coyotes howled before

tearing apart a rabbit; at 4 a.m.

a baker slides dough into an oven:
the aroma rises from the basement kiln—

and, as you inhale, it drizzles on deck:
three miles from the coastline,

you scattered ashes, and swirling

on waves, they formed a gray,
black-speckled cloud before sinking—

at the beach, you screwed
an umbrella pole into the sand,

heard cry and cry but saw nothing:

then a piping plover, skirting
toward the water, revealed,

behind rocks, four speckled eggs;
after replanting the pole, sitting under

an umbrella, you felt how a skin

separated you from death, how death
contoured the pause between exhale

and inhale, how it flowered inside
the bougainvillea blooming by a glass

door and sparked the white page

into light; and, as glass molecules
slow as the temperature cools

yet never lock into crystal patterns,
you feel how *once* never locks,

how it vibrates, quickens inside you:

then you level with a taxi driver
swerving between trucks, level

with a potter who mashes a bowl
back into a ball, level with a magpie

that congregates and squawks

with other magpies over a corpse
before flying off, and when you hike

up the ridge, dew rising into
the morning, you ride the flex

of your muscles as you lift the gate—

Acknowledgments

Grateful acknowledgment is made to the editors of the following publications, in which these poems, sometimes in earlier versions, first appeared:

Academy of American Poets "Poem-a-Day" (Poets.org): "First Snow," "Stilling to North," "Unpacking a Globe," "White Sands"

The Asian American Literary Review: "Water Calligraphy" (reprint)

Boston Review: "Courtyard Fire"

Conjunctions: "Water Calligraphy"

FIELD: "In the Bronx," "Winter Stars"

The Harvard Advocate: "Dawn Redwood"

The Hollins Critic: "Traversal"

Kenyon Review: "The Glass Constellation," "Python Skin," "Sight Lines"

Mānoa: "Sprang"

The Massachusetts Review: "Cloud Hands"

Narrative: "Lichen Song"

The Nation: "Salt Song"

New England Review: "Xeriscape"

The New Republic: "The Far Norway Maples"

Orion: "The Radiant's"

Ploughshares: "Black Center"

Plume (online): "Doppler Effect," "Sprang," "Talisman"

Plume Anthology of Poetry (vols. 3, 4, 5): "Transfigurations," "Under a Rising Moon," "Light Echoes," respectively.

Poet Lore: "Adamant"

Poetry: "Kintsugi," "Net Light"

Poetry Daily (online): "Talisman"

Terrain.org: "Adamant," "Traversal"(reprints)

Vallum (Canada): "Hole"

*Writing on the Edge: "This Is the Writing, the
    Speaking of the Dream,"* "Westbourne Street"

"White Sands" was commissioned by the Academy of American Poets and funded by a National Endowment for the Arts Imagine Your Parks grant.

"Black Center" was printed as a letterpress broadside by Thomas Leech at the Press at the Palace of the Governors, Santa Fe, 2018. It was published in an edition of 120 copies, 80 of which are reserved for the Codex Foundation's special project: *EXTRACTION: Art on the Edge of the Abyss.*

"Sight Lines" appeared in the anthology *Monticello in Mind: Fifty Contemporary Poems on Jefferson,* edited by Lisa Russ Spaar (University of Virginia Press, 2016).

I am grateful for the Jackson Poetry Prize, which was a great help in writing this book, and want to thank Poets & Writers, the Liana Foundation, and John and Susan Jackson.

"Courtyard Fire," "First Snow," and "Sight Lines" appeared in *The Jackson Poetry Prize: Celebrating the Winners, Volume II* (Poets & Writers Inc., 2016).

Thank you, Mei-mei Berssenbrugge, Dana Levin, Carol Moldaw, and Jim Moore, for close readings of these poems.

Thank you, Michael Wiegers, for your unflagging support of my work through the years.

Thank you, David Caligiuri and Alison Lockhart, for your meticulous copyediting; thank you, Valerie B. Caldwell, for your gorgeous design; and thanks to Joseph Bednarik, George Knotek, John Pierce, Laura Buccieri, Emily Grise, Elaina Ellis, Sara Ritter, Rio Cortez, Janeen Armstrong, Randy Sturgis, and Margaret Kirk at Copper Canyon Press.

Notes

pp. 8–9   "Water Calligraphy" (*dì shū*): at sunrise in China, elderly men often go to public parks, dip brushes in water, and write calligraphy on the slate walkways. As the water evaporates, the characters disappear.

p. 15   "Cloud Hands" is for JoAnna Schoon.

p. 35   In "Courtyard Fire," the italicized lines are a condensation of a sentence from Karl Marx's "A Contribution to the Critique of Hegel's *Philosophy of Right*" (1884).

p. 42   A Japanese term, *kintsugi* ("golden joinery") is the art of repairing broken pottery with gold-dusted lacquer.

p. 45   *This is the writing, the speaking of the dream* is Dennis Tedlock's translation of the beginning of a series of glyphs on a Mayan ceramic vessel.

p. 50   "Dawn Redwood" is in memory of C.D. Wright. The italicized line is from her poem "Floating Trees."

pp. 57–58 The italicized lines are from *The Art of War* by Sun Tzu, translated by Samuel B. Griffith (New York: Oxford University Press, 1963).

About the Author

Arthur Sze is a poet, translator, and editor. He is the author of ten books of poetry and is a professor emeritus at the Institute of American Indian Arts. His poems have been translated into eleven languages, including Chinese, Dutch, German, Korean, Italian, and Spanish. A recipient of the Jackson Poetry Prize from Poets & Writers, two fellowships from the National Endowment for the Arts, a Guggenheim Fellowship, a Howard Foundation Fellowship, a Lannan Literary Award, an American Book Award, a Lila Wallace-Reader's Digest Writers' Award, as well as five grants from the Witter Bynner Foundation for Poetry, Sze was the first poet laureate of Santa Fe, where he lives with his wife, Carol Moldaw. From 2012–2017, he was a chancellor of the Academy of American Poets and, in 2017, was elected a fellow of the American Academy of Arts and Sciences.

Poetry is vital to language and living. Since 1972, Copper Canyon Press has published extraordinary poetry from around the world to engage the imaginations and intellects of readers, writers, booksellers, librarians, teachers, students, and donors.

WE ARE GRATEFUL FOR THE MAJOR SUPPORT PROVIDED BY:

THE PAUL G. ALLEN
FAMILY FOUNDATION

Anonymous (3)
Jill Baker and Jeffrey Bishop
Anne and Geoffrey Barker
Donna and Matt Bellew
John Branch
Diana Broze
The Beatrice R. and Joseph A. Coleman Foundation, Inc.
Laurie and Oskar Eustis
Mimi Gardner Gates
Nancy Gifford
Gull Industries, Inc. on behalf of William True
The Trust of Warren A. Gummow
Petunia Charitable Fund and advisor Elizabeth Hebert
Bruce Kahn
Phil Kovacevich and Eric Wechsler
Lakeside Industries, Inc.
on behalf of Jeanne Marie Lee
Maureen Lee and Mark Busto